MOMMY'S HATS

By
Rhonda Zweber

Eloquent Books
New York, New York

Eloquent Books

An imprint of AEG Publishing Group

845 Third Avenue, 6th Floor - 6016

New York, NY 10022

www.eloquentbooks.com

ISBN 978-1-60860-204-9

Printed in the United States of America

Book Design: Linda W. Rigsbee

To Val for loving me with and without

To Ashley for your quiet concern

To Hailey for your words of encouragement

and

To Sally for your sweet innocence

and giving me a reason to share this book with the world.

Hi, my name is Sally. I'm five years old and my mommy has a bump in her breast. She says it's called "breast cancer". I asked where the bump is but Mommy says I can't see it because it's inside her breast.

Mommy told me that she was going to have to take very strong medicine to make the bump smaller. This medicine is called "chemotherapy." I'll call it chemo because that's easier to say. She also said that the medicine might make her hair fall out and might make her tummy sick. This medicine isn't like the cough medicine I take, so, my hair won't fall out.

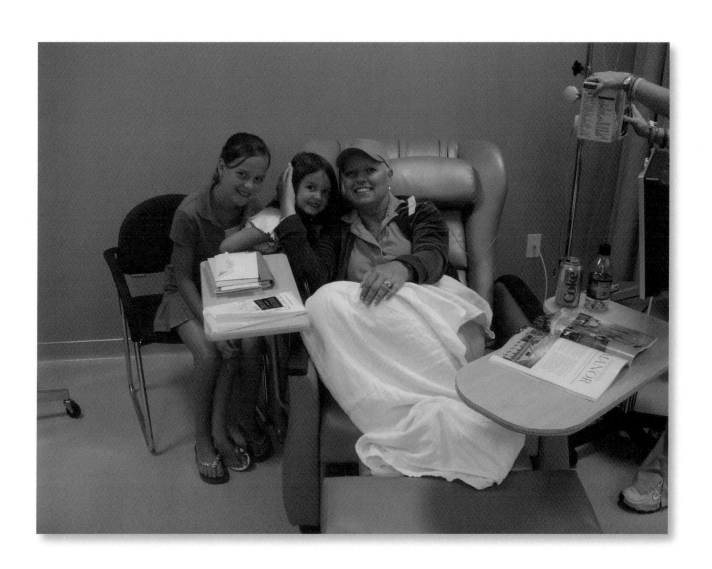

Mommy had to get another bump to help get the medicine in her body. She said it's called a "port". I can see this bump.

"She needs this bump to get rid of the other bump," I told my friend, as I pointed to Mommy's port and then her breast.

Mommy has to go to the doctor a lot to make sure everything is going right. I don't mind because I get to go to my grandma's and grandpa's house or play with my cousin, Morgan.

After mommy gets her medicine, she sleeps a lot. She says it helps make the medicine work better. I check on her to see if she needs me for anything.

At first, Mommy got sick in her tummy and couldn't play with me. Daddy had to bring her food on a tray in her bedroom. I asked her, "If I hug you, will you throw up on me?" She said "No." I was glad. After a couple of days, she felt better and could play games with me again.

Mommy needs to take a lot of naps. She says it keeps her strong and gives her energy to play with me or go places. I sometimes take naps with her. Mommy felt good enough to celebrate our birthdays at my aunt and uncle's house.

One day, Mommy's hair started to come out. So, we went to get her hair cut really, really short. She looked like a boy, and I

didn't like it. Then, I felt her head and it felt like a fuzzy bear. I wanted to touch it all the time!

After Mommy got her hair all cut off, she had to wear a hat when we went places. She didn't wear a hat when we were at home. She said she would forget that her hair was so short until she looked into a mirror. She has

a lot of different hats to wear. We like to try them all on to see how we look.

One day, Mommy wanted me to come upstairs and when I went into her bathroom, she had white stuff all over her head! She was shaving

her head so that it would be smooth and wouldn't be itchy anymore. She asked me if I wanted to shave part of her

head. At first, I was scared that I would hurt her, but she said I wouldn't so I did it. It was neat to help Mommy shave her head. Daddy and my big sister, Hailey, helped, too.

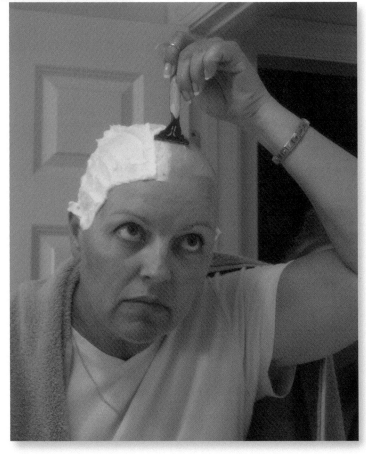

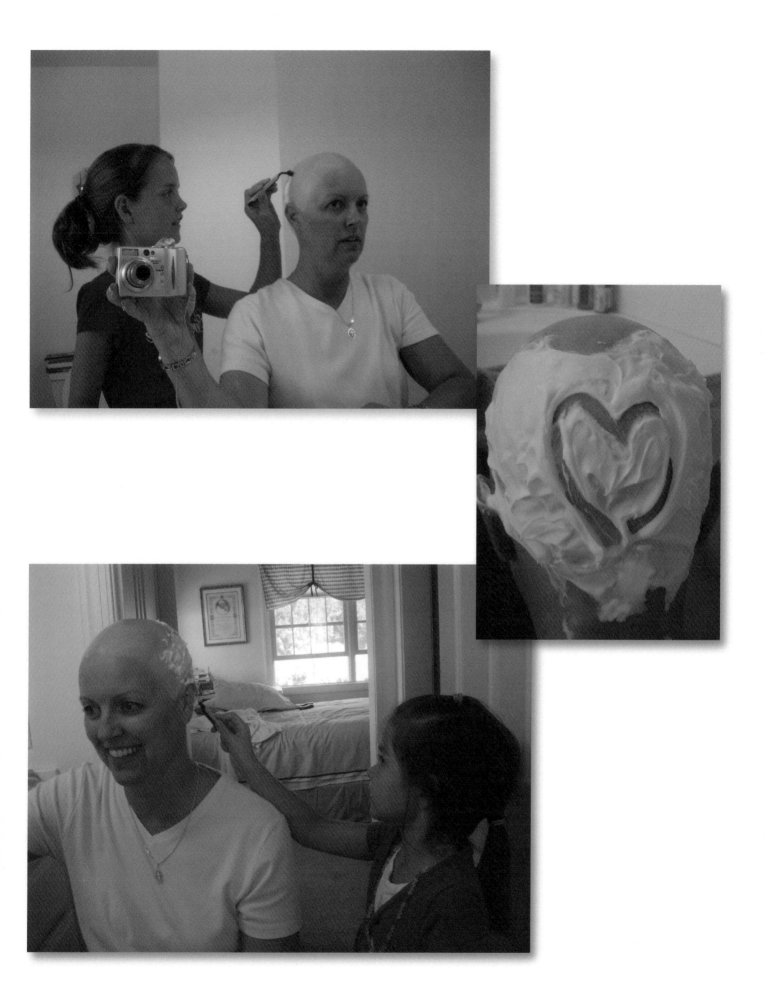

I sometimes forget that Mommy has breast cancer. She doesn't look sick. I love the times when she doesn't have to stay in bed all day.

When Mommy was done taking her medicine, she had to have an operation to get rid of the bump. It's called a "lumpectomy". When she told me about it, I made a funny face because it sounded icky. She said she would be sleeping so it wouldn't hurt. She didn't have to stay overnight at the hospital and I'm glad because I would have missed her. Mommy had a tube coming out of her body to drain the blood from her operation. It looked really icky and she wanted to keep really still because it hurt a little, and she was afraid it might get pulled out if she moved too much.

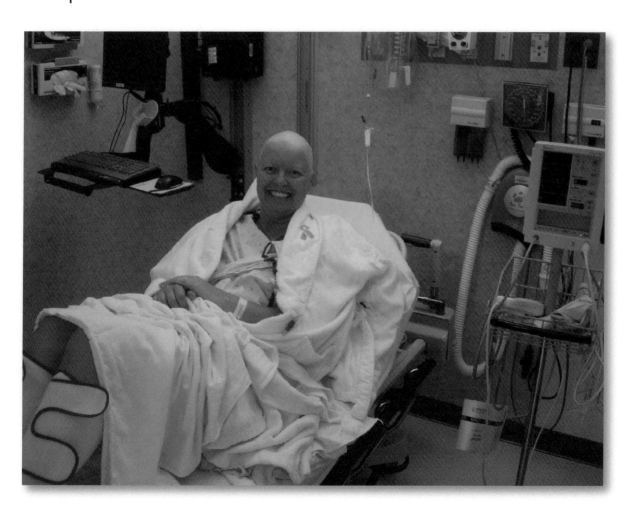

The day after the surgery, Mommy got a phone call from the hospital telling her that there was more cancer in her breast and she needed to have another operation. This time the doctor had to take both of Mommy's breasts. I didn't know what that meant at first. I felt sad for her because she was really sad.

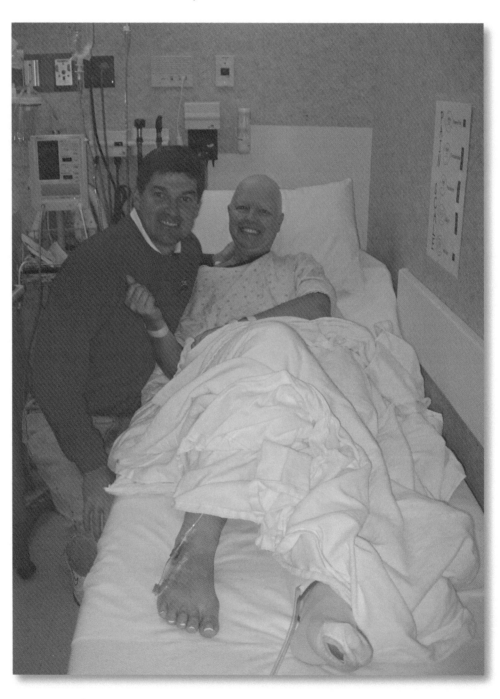

When Mommy woke up from her operation, I got to go see her. She was very sleepy and didn't feel very good, so I didn't stay very long. But when she came home the next day, she felt better. She went right up to her bedroom and stayed there for a few days. She looked sad, so I tried to make her happy. I told her she looked pretty.

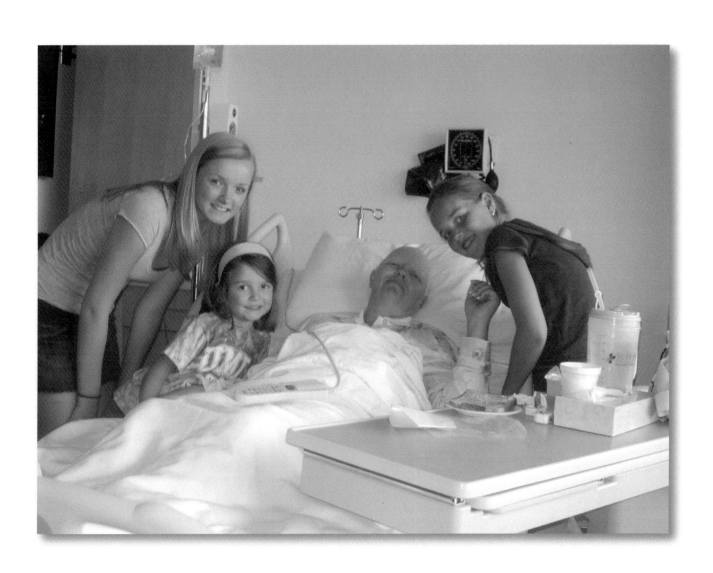

I asked Mommy if I could see her breasts. She said they weren't there anymore but I could see her bandage, so she showed it to me. Her bandage was wrapped around her body and she had two tubes this time. I asked her why she had two tubes. She said there was one for each breast. It was really hard to hug Mommy with two tubes in, but I was really, really careful. I still wanted to snuggle with her; I just had to lie really still so I wouldn't bump Mommy's tubes. When she went to the doctor to get her tubes out, she came home with new breasts. They weren't her real breasts; they were pretend. I wanted to see them, too. She showed me. She called them "breast forms." When we were at the store, I told Mommy that it didn't look like she didn't have any breasts.

She told me, "Thank you, but we aren't supposed to talk about it in front of other people."

"Why?" I asked.

Mommy said, "Other people don't know that I…"

I tried to finish her sentence by saying, "Have cancer?"

"They probably know that I have cancer," she said, "but don't know that my breasts are gone."

At church on Sunday, I prayed for Mommy's hair and breasts to grow back. Mommy said that her hair will grow back but her breasts won't. She told me that she will have more operations to make new breasts after she is done taking her medicine.

When it was time for me to go to kindergarten, I was a little sad for Mommy. I was going to miss being with her all day. I figured she would be OK and probably take naps while I was at school.

She had to take medicine in her port four more times. This time, instead of getting sick in her tummy, she got an owie pain in her legs. I asked if I could rub her legs to make them feel better, but they hurt Mommy too much for anyone to touch them. But, she liked it when I massaged her shoulders.

Mommy's hair didn't fall out this time but she had owies on her head from the medicine, so she wore her hats again. I wore my hat so I looked just like her. When her owies went away and

her hair was getting longer, she colored her hair brown. I told her I wouldn't like her unless she had her gray hair. I really didn't mean that I wouldn't like her, but I like her better with gray hair. I hope I didn't make her feel bad when I said that. She's had gray hair for as long as I can remember.

As Mommy got better after taking her chemo, she waited to see if her eyebrows and eyelashes would fall out again, like they did the first time after having chemo. They fell out even after she was done taking the medicine. She kept saying, "They're hanging in there!" But last week, she saw that her eyelashes were falling out. She wasn't too sad about it because she said there wasn't anything she could do about it and they will grow back anyway. I saw an eyelash on Mommy's nose and I let her make a wish and then blow it off my finger. I think she wished that her eyelashes wouldn't fall out anymore. I thought of all of the wishes she could get if she made one every time one fell out!

Mommy's next operation was to make new breasts. I don't really get how it works, but she said the doctor will put balloons in her breasts and fill them with water. She calls them "expanders." She had to see the doctor every week to put water in the balloons until they were full. It made Mommy really sore, so she would lie really still and I read books to her.

I asked her a lot of questions so that I would know things. I asked, "Do you have two water balloons or one?"

"One," she said.

I asked, "What color are they?"

"White," she said.

I asked, "How do they keep from leaking when the doctor puts more water in them?"

"There is a special valve that she pokes the needle through with the water," Mommy said.

There is a lot to know!

Mommy's next treatment was called "radiation." She had to lie really still on a table, with her arms over her head. It was hard to lay still for a long time at first, but it got better with time. She had to go to the hospital thirty times all together. I went a couple of times.

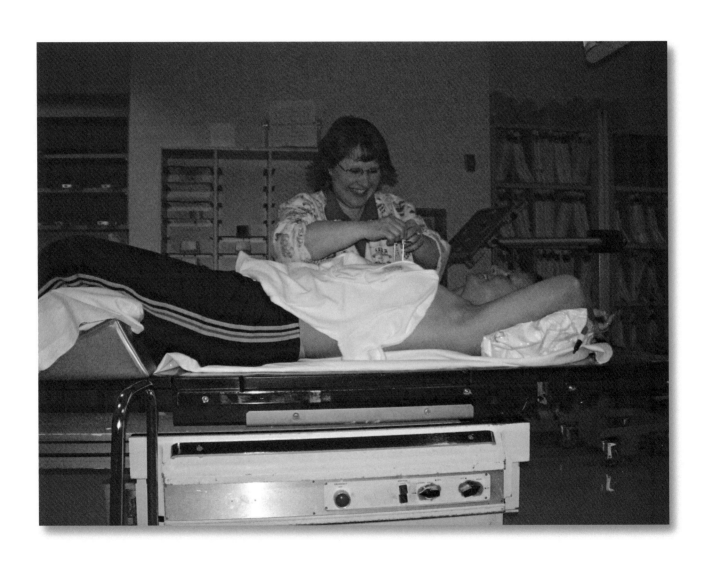

Mommy's skin looked like she got sunburned and I helped put special lotion on her back where she couldn't reach.

When her skin got better, she was able to exercise again. We signed up for Tae Kwon Do and I loved it. I was really good at it. We still practice a lot in the kitchen.

Mommy and I got our feet washed on Holy Thursday. I was a little scared to go up on the altar, but I was brave and did it. Mommy got her feet washed first by Father Tom, and then it was my turn. The water was really warm and it felt good.

I sat on Mommy's lap and I leaned on her port. I sat up and asked her if she still had her wart! I forgot for a second that it's called a port. Silly me.

Then it was time to plan Mommy's party to thank all the people who helped us through Mommy's cancer. We decorated the house and garage with a lot of pink!

On Mother's Day, I was able to walk with Mommy. She had ninety-six people on her team! I got to ride on my cousins, Emily's and Ben's backs. I got to carry the sign, too.

The next day was another one of Mommy's surgeries. She had to be at the hospital really early, so I gave her a big hug and kiss before I went to bed. This operation took out her expanders and put in nice breasts. She calls them "implants". She said that these would feel and look like real breasts. She also had another operation that will help her from getting another cancer. She had two operations in one day! She had to stay overnight at the hospital, and I got to sleep with Daddy. Mommy was home and in her bed when I got home from school. I got my blankie and snuggled up to her as close I could without hurting her. I've gotten really good at being close to Mommy without bumping her.

Now, I'm six years old. I've had quite a year. I've learned a lot about cancer and how to take care of Mommy. I thought I was going to feel scared but I didn't. Whenever I wondered about something, I asked Mommy and she would explain it to me. She needs to see the doctor every few months until I'm ten years old. I'm really glad that Mommy feels better now. We're going to have a lot of fun this summer!

LaVergne, TN USA
21 December 2009
167669LV00002B